Look Back at Old Abertillery

Malcolm Thomas
& Ray Morris

Foreword by
Roy Jenkins, BBC Wales

Volume 1

Old Bakehouse Publications

Abertillery

First published in May 1999
Reprinted in June 2001
Reprinted in June 2003

ISBN 1 874538 37 9

Published in the U.K. by
Old Bakehouse Publications
Church Street,
Abertillery, Gwent NP13 1EA
Telephone: 01495 212600 Fax: 01495 216222
Email: oldbakehouseprint@btopenworld.com

Made and printed in the UK
by J.R. Davies (Printers) Ltd.

British Library Cataloguing in Publication Data: a catalogue
record for this book is available from the British Library.

Foreword

by

Roy Jenkins, BBC Wales

To my great delight, I discovered my father looking out at me from one of the pictures in this book. It's 25 years since he died, and I never knew the photograph existed.

He would have been surprised to find himself in these pages. And so, I imagine, would many of the people we meet here, since this is not a chronicle of those alleged to be "the great" and "the good". It's just a tiny selection of those who have worked and played, raised families, taught, traded, prayed in Abertillery in the past century (some very great and some very good among them; and others not so ...).

This is a book to stir memories of things long gone: Ralph's and Griffin's buses; the Bon Marché and the Pontlottyn; the Gaiety and the Pavilion; and, yes, there really was a railway station. And, of course, the people: in pubs and clubs, in choirs and cricket teams, and on the streets in their thousands for the churches' Whitsun walks.

We need records like this not simply to feed our nostalgia, but to remind us where we've come from, and to give us a clearer perspective on where we are now.

These pages offer us glimpses of the ways in which the valleys have been shaped by suffering: the sheer grind of coal mine and tinplate works; the desperation which prompted a future king to declare, "Something must be done"; and the sacrifice of war (I had never realised that Abertillery's war memorial contains a staggering 601 names from two world wars).

They also point to a town whose rich sense of community once had an active allegiance to the Christian faith close to its heart. That's where even those of us now in exile have come from. There's much to learn. And much to humble us.

Contents

Introduction

More than one photographic book has been published in recent years portraying the life and times of Abertillery and yet there appears as always, even more previously unpublished material to savour. The authors have delved into their extensive collections of old postcards and photographs and with the help of additional material kindly provided by some local colleagues,this first volume in a new series of books has been produced.

Like the rest of South Wales, prior to the discovery and exploitation of coal, the district was once a green and pleasant land occupied solely by a small number of hill farmers. By the mid nineteenth century, coal was to become central to the economy of the whole of the western valley with the population of Abertillery rising to an astonishing 39,000 during the peak period of the 1920s. At this time the town was surpassed in size only by Newport in the county of Monmouthshire, subsequently acquiring its own Parliamentary seat, providing a number of prominent politicians and the largest constituency elected majority in the land.

It was of course, not only the pleasant land and the fuel that lay beneath it that was exploited, this exploitation was extended to the men, women and children who in earlier years were obliged to toil beneath the earth just to survive. The true price of coal will never be determined but early history from medieval times makes interesting reading. During the reign of King Edward I the inhabitants of London petitioned the king against the growing use of coal, declaring it to be a public nuisance corrupting the air with stink and smoke. The king thus prohibited its use in preference to the burning of wood, eventually declaring it a capital offence and indeed records exist of a man being publicly hanged for daring to use the wretched fuel!

This book however does not dwell purely on an important industrial past but looks at many other aspects through the medium of photographs. The street scenes, some in colour for the first time, provide evidence of previous prosperity with the number of shops and long forgotten trades that once adorned the town. Amongst those past traders were such business folk as Harry Campion the artificial teeth maker, Joseph Harris the sugar boiler, Gwen Hepple the milliner, Vaughan and Sons the saddlers to say nothing of the numerous ironmongers, wheelwrights and chimney sweeps, all one-time important professions which mean little to today's generations. There should however be many readers who will recall that Abertillery was blessed with various sources of entertainment for all tastes. For instance there were four cinemas to choose from, The Pavilion and Empress in Carlyle Street, The Palace in Carmel Street and the precarious Gaiety built over the River Ebbw. For true theatricals, nothing in the valley could compare with The Metropole, the Operatic Society having delighted audiences here since the year 1916. The town has never been deficient in talent from a number of quarters and there will be a number of familiar faces to be seen on some of the photographs included in this book.

For the faithful of all denominations, there were more than twenty places of worship to choose from in days gone by and some of the pictures in Chapter Four help to remind us of this. It is not only the churches and chapels that have quietly disappeared and been forgotten as the years have passed by. Many once-familiar scenes around the town have changed almost beyond recognition and attention is drawn to the final chapter. The photographs included here speak volumes and deserve careful study to remind us once again of the continuing changes facing Abertillery as we approach this, the end of the twentieth century.

CHAPTER 1

In and around the town

1. This is how the middle of Somerset Street looked in 1904 with the three-storey shop The Bon Marché occupying much of it. Competition was intense for large valley shops and the attraction at this former Abertillery store was to pay the customers' train fare if they were to spend £1 or more. The company also owned branches in Bargoed, Ebbw Vale, Abergavenny and Hereford.

2. Looking up Commercial Street in about 1903 when it was a safe haven for pedestrians. In the background can be seen the Commercial Hotel and the building on the bottom left is now occupied by the Midland Bank.

3. Another picture of Commercial Street, this time looking downwards during the early years of the twentieth century, and a single gas lamp provides the street's lighting requirements outside the Bon Marché. Most of the buildings seen here still stand, with the exception of the three-storeyed structure at the bottom of the picture which may be remembered as The Globe Inn.

4. A view across Somerset Street from the junction with Commercial Street, and the period has moved forward to the early 1930s. Two former shops to be seen in the background are Holmans the newsagents and Simons for furniture. The latter is now a branch of Woolworths.

5. This view of Somerset Street is from the mid 1920s and was taken close to the Police Station, which may be seen on the left. The horse and cart is parked outside Mortimers shop on the right and close by, is the former Methodist Church. Another popular shop nearby, but just out of the picture, was Pauls the music shop with a reputation for being able to supply any piece of music one could possibly think of !

6. Vivian Street before necessary 'speed humps' were introduced. On the left is the St. John's Ambulance Hall which was used as a first aid training centre by the former colliers of Abertillery. Also to be seen on the lower left is the old gasometer. The street was much quieter then, and a lady resident finds time to shake the doormat.

7. Foundry Bridge, the picture having been taken during the early 1960s when Tillery Street Methodist Church, seen on the left, was still active. This church was the victim of arsonists and subsequently demolished as unsafe in the 1980s. In the foreground is the Esso garage, since gone, but the large building in the centre is the Liberal Club which is still frequented.

8. A colourful Church Street of 1908 with a few shops selling goods from the past, such as Ormstons for pianos with Edwards the ironmongers on the opposite side, displaying a fine selection of tin buckets.

9. Abertillery's former substantial General Post Office in Castle Street. Outside can be seen a drinking fountain, probably welcomed by a weary horse with its milk cart. The building was in later years converted into The Cotton Wood Cafe and owned by Mr. Ron Jones of Jones's Bus Company. The building on the right used to house the local Council Offices.

10. Commercial Street with a crowd of pedestrians looking at a cameraman of 1905. On the left is a ladies' costumiers, or clothes shop which might sound more familiar these days. This was Davies's shop which stood at the entrance to the Arcade.

11. The often photographed Church Street, on this occasion in about 1920. Amongst the shops with their sun-blinds, is the old chemists belonging to the Prichard family, who had been Abertillery's purveyor of medicines since the nineteenth century; the present-day owners still retain the Prichard name for business purposes. At the end of the street on the right is the former Trinity Presbyterian Chapel which was built in 1878 and is nowadays a carpet store. Further along in Tillery Street can be seen the once imposing steeple of the Methodist Chapel, opened in 1906 and serving the town for almost 75 years before destruction. All was not lost however and a replacement Methodist Church can now be found close by in Powell Street.

12. The early years of transport as seen in Somerset Street. A traditional horse and cart faces in one direction and a prized motor car, complete with carbide lamps and solid tyres in the other. The former Bell Inn and Edward Purnell the stationers are seen on the left.

13. The carts are stood outside a shop in Church Street belonging to George Jones and Son and called, 'The Peoples Music and Furniture Warehouse'. Next door is a boot and shoe shop and this is approximately where the shoe shop is in Church Street today.

14. A pre-war view of the Cock and Chick Mountain from the Rose Heyworth side. The housing developments of Arael View and the Rose Heyworth Estate have yet to be built. In the upper right can be seen the old quarry and Brutens Farm.

15. A very early photograph looking up the hill towards the Foundry Bridge. The first bridge was built in the 1890s and acquired its name from the iron and brass foundry which was situated just below. The foundry was opened here in 1874 by Mr. Henry Ward Williams of Alma Street and over the years, developed into an important company and employer for the town to be better known as Warwills.

16. Another look at Somerset Street and this scene makes interesting comparison with picture number 12. The car is a little more up to date and Purnell's shop has now become a showroom for the gas company. The Bell Inn on the left, was accessible from Somerset Street and Market Street, it having two bars known to locals as 'Top Bell' and 'Bottom Bell'.

17. All quiet on The Foundry Bridge ninety years ago, the picture having been taken from Division Street looking towards Alma Street.

18. A Leyland bus belonging to the Griffin Motor Company is seen opposite the former Station Hotel and en route to Newbridge. Griffin buses with their red and cream livery were a familiar sight around the western valley, the Brynmawr-based company always in keen competition with Ralphs of Abertillery.

19. This time a passenger boards a Ralphs bus of AEC manufacture outside Howards Bakery in Division Street. Led by the senior member of the family Mr. S. Ralph, the company was originally engaged in the manufacture of a much acclaimed ginger beer, before developing into a transport business. The bus company was formed in 1901 initially providing horse-drawn travel around the area before the arrival of the first motor vehicle, a Napier charabanc in 1914. Ralphs buses with their distinctive black and yellow livery, were to be seen on the roads until the 1950s before this independent firm was eventually absorbed by the Red and White Company.

20. The top end of Oak Street as it looked in the early 1900s. The houses on the upper left have since been demolished to make way for a car parking area and Oak Street Garage now stands where the old gas lamp standard is.

21. Another view of early 1900s Oak Street, this time the lower end. On the right-hand side of the street is one of the town's Temperance (no alcohol licence) Hotels; this particular one being opened by John Thomas Buckley and his wife Mary in 1892. The hotel was to become the first headquarters of the relatively young Abertillery Rugby Club.

22. Market Street in 1909 with the impressive Market Hall which was built in 1892. Beneath the hall is the old London Joint City and Midland Bank and further along, the handcart stands outside Amarille Jackson's confectionery shop.

23. An interesting photograph showing the demolition of the Pavilion Cinema in progress. The tall building on the left, with slates still on its roof is another cinema, The Gaiety. This former Abertillery picture house was situated in Bridge Street and was built over the river. The Gaiety also, was to be pulled down later and these days, the town is without a cinema, where once there were four.

24. An early general view of the town with Glandwr Street in the foreground. In the centre can be seen the railway lines and the bridge over the tracks near Oak Street.

25. This scene is taken from a 1920s postcard captioned 'Station Approach Abertillery'. Today, a little help may be needed in recognising the area; the advertisement boards on the left now form the location of the library.

26. It is 1905 and a young resident of Glandwr Street stares at the photographer. To the left would be the entrance to the lower park and a little further up on the hillside, the old Blaina Road.

27. This view may not appear to be too clear, the result of the amount of industrial haze and smoke that once clouded over Abertillery. Looking south, the picture shows part of Penybont and the colliery.

28. Castle Street, looking towards the Bush Hotel. As will be seen, this is where the Fire Station was located before the new premises were built on the old railway sidings, at the bottom of Station Hill. Locals may also recall the old Fire Station being used as a small clothing factory for a period after closure.

29. This is how the general view overlooking the town appeared in 1937. Close scrutiny of the picture will show many long-gone buildings from the centre and particularly, the overhead buckets which were used to deposit waste on the mountain top.

30. A picture taken from the top of Gaen Street, Blaenau Gwent in about 1906; the street in early years and for some unknown reason, being given the local nickname of 'Cardiff Road'. On the right is the Post Office, which at the time was also the local grocery store in the capable hands of Mr. Fred Fielding.

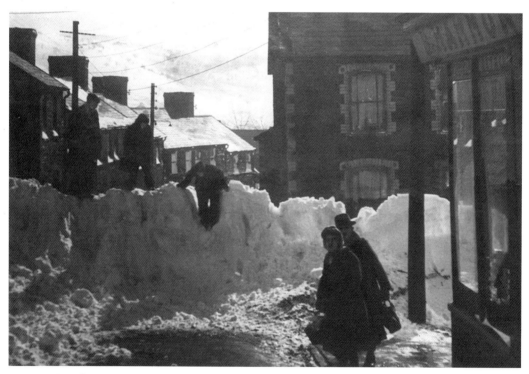

31. Another picture from Blaenau Gwent, taken outside Bryn Hammond's shop. Heavy snow sometimes brings things to a standstill in the town and on this occasion, the period is thought to be the hard winter of 1963.

32.   Alma Street seen in days when there were houses present on both sides of the road. The shop seen on the bottom right was the popular sweet shop owned by Mr. Terrett. Elders may remember that further up the road was the fruit and veg shop belonging to Mr. Jim Arnold; it was here on New Year's Day that Mr. Arnold would give the local children a traditional sixpence.

33.   A view looking up Cwm Cottage Road in about 1915 with a fine example of old Abertillery's street gas lighting on the corner of Princess Street.

34. The general picture of Abertillery in the 1920s, with a large waste tip in the centre and a few buildings which are no longer to be seen, such as the old Council Offices on the corner of King Street. The area where the tip is, housed a centre providing meals for the children of the unemployed during the great depression of the 1930s.

35. Looking towards the Cock and Chick Mountain sixty years ago. In the centre of the photograph is the old County School which had been built in 1897.

36. Gwern Berthi Road Cwmtillery and the men stood on the road will be on their way home after a shift at Cwmtillery Colliery. Their blackened faces show that there was no such luxury as a pithead baths in those days. They can also be seen carrying blocks of wood in their arms; this was a 'perk' for the miners of Cwmtillery, who were allowed one block per day as firewood for the home.

37. St. Paul's Church and the villas at Cwmtillery. The villas at one time were occupied by some of the managers of Cwmtillery Colliery. The long building in the centre of the picture was the church hall where many of the local fêtes and festivities were held.

38. This concluding photograph in Chapter One may prove a little mystifying to some. It was taken at the end of James Street before the offending waste tip which overlooked the area was removed. Much was done in later years to improve the appearance, with a landscaped park area being opened by King Edward VIII in 1936.

CHAPTER 2

An Industrious Past

39. This chapter opens with a typical scene at Cwmtillery Colliery, with Mr. Joseph Mills on the left accompanied by two workmates. Mr. Mills (grandfather of co-author Ray Morris) was better known as 'Joe The Saw' and he, like many others, came from the rural Midlands to seek a better living in an industrious South Wales, during the early years of the twentieth century.

40. Cwmtillery Colliery as seen from the west side when it was a thriving concern. The first two shafts were sunk here in the year 1850, with an additional sinking to a depth of 783 feet opening in 1858. Peak production of coal at Cwmtillery was during the period leading up World War One in 1914 with output reaching 11,500 tons per week.

41. Another view of the colliery in later years, by which time the rows of houses had been demolished. The British coal industry was nationalised in 1947 and prior to that date, Cwmtillery had known a number of different owners with a total amount of coal extracted by them estimated at 30 million tons. The fate of the British coal industry was probably sealed following the industrial dispute of 1974; the country was forced into a three day working week for nearly two months and the politicians of the day did not forget. The last coal was brought to the surface at Cwmtillery in 1982 and 132 years of mining came to an end.

42. As evidenced by the collection of photographs included in this book, Abertillery was once rich with coal workings. This picture is of Rose Heyworth Pit which was situated between Abertillery and Bournville. Coal was first lifted here in 1872 and as with Cwmtillery, it was to operate for well over 100 years before finally closing in the mid 1980s.

43. Rose Heyworth Colliery was in later years to be re-named Abertillery New Mine. For a number of years it was connected to South Griffin Colliery in Blaina and also Cwmtillery for ventilation purposes. Rose Heyworth and Cwmtillery were eventually merged with a new drift driven to raise coal from both workings.

44. A 'Jolly Boys Outing' has been planned for these Abertillery miners during a day of rest in the 1930s. Notice how nearly everyone appears to be wearing the same style of cap and a few with the traditional scarved necks!

45. Workers at Cwmtillery pose for a photograph alongside the locomotive 'Caradog' and are armed with sprags, ready to stop the coal-laden wagons. The year is 1956 and one of the lads positively identified is Arthur Sweet who is seen second from the left.

46. The Gray Pit, which was owned by Powells Tillery Steam Coal Company operated for about 50 years until closure in 1938. It was however used as a mining training centre until the 1947 Nationalisation. As with most of the pits in the district, there is little remaining evidence of coal mining, Gray Pit now being the site of the Comprehensive School.

47. More evidence of busy industrial locomotion in Abertillery is provided here. This engine was used for shunting materials in and out of the tin works, the picture having been taken on the lines just below the Castle Hotel.

48. Abertillery Park would appear to the setting for a mass meeting of local miners some 80 or 90 years ago. It was of course the dispute between the miners, the then private coal-owners and the Government which led to the great General Strike throughout the country in 1926. This event heralded a depression that was to haunt the valleys for another ten years at least.

49. Some workers are pictured 'on top' at Cwmtillery Colliery and a few names have been identified. Third from the left is Ted Price who was later to become Chairman of Cwmtillery Lodge. First on the right is Les Gilbert and stood next to him is Roy Jones.

50. A photograph dating from about 1920 of some local miners about to take refreshment at the South Wales Inn Cwmtillery. Second from the right is Mr. James Legge with appropriate attire for the period; a flat cap, sturdy lace-up boots and a treasured watch with chain.

51. A chance to see the interior of the local Remploy factory where employees are busy at their machines making industrial gloves. The factory was built on an old part of the park and commenced production in January 1951, providing jobs for some seventy disabled men and women who had previously been given no proper opportunity in the workplace.

52. Once common sights throughout South Wales and beyond, were the tips of industrial spoils. Here is some 1960s mountain scenery at Abertillery, only to be marred by the large coal-waste tip belonging to Rose Heyworth Colliery. At the bottom of the picture can be seen the houses of Glandwr Street.

53. A close-up view of the workings at Cwmtillery during the 1920s. Unaware of what the long term future of the colliery would be, huge investment was made here in 1977, with the longest and most advanced underground man-riding system in South Wales being installed. Travelling some 3000 metres underground, this new seven carriage manrider could now carry men directly to the coalface in 12 minutes compared with a previous 40 minute slog on foot.

54./55. Both of these photographs are of the Abertillery Tinworks. A very old company, it was originally started in 1846 and provided work for 111 years. After closure, part of the premises were occupied by another well-known local engineering company, Warwills. In 1998 the site was razed to the ground to make way for a familiar supermarket.

56. The platforms of Abertillery Station, looking north towards Blaina in 1919 when Mr. Albert Webber held the important post of stationmaster; the last gentleman to fill the position before closure was Mr. Ernest Jones. Freight trains frequented Abertillery for a few years after passenger traffic ceased, the goods yard however was eventually closed in April 1969.

57. Looking south along the unique 'S' shaped platforms, the next stop being Six Bells Halt. Abertillery was a commodious station at one time, catering for up to twenty passenger trains per day in each direction. The much-loved steam locomotives gave way to diesel units in the late 1950s, but not for long; the last passenger train left Abertillery on April 30th 1962.

58. A town scene from about 1907, looking towards Castle Street. Just visible in the foreground is the old gas works, which was owned by Abertillery Council, the first such works being built in 1867. The wonder of electrictity was introduced to the town in 1901, being supplied by a new generating station built at Glandwr Aberbeeg.

59./60. Here is more evidence of the collection of pits that once circled the town, and the importance coal was to play in the local economy. This is Penybont and the scenes show rows of wagons marked, Powell's Tillery Steam Coal Company of Cardiff, the colliery owners at the time. The houses in the background belong to Tillery Road.

CHAPTER 3

Trading Places

61. Two of the town's prestige shops faced each other on the corner of Somerset Street and Commercial Street, they were Morgan and Francis's Pontlottyn Shop and The Bon Marché. This 1898 picture shows that the Bon Marché was still a single-storey building.

62. Attentive and potential customers listen to the persuasions of a market trader during the 1960s. The dealing is seen when the open-air stalls were in Mitre Street.

63. The former fish and vegetable shop of James Barter and Sons, which was a popular corner shop in Somerset Street. Like many such businesses, it too had a nickname and was always known to locals as 'Fatty Barters'. This shop is now the Chinese Takeaway.

64./65. Looking through the Arcade 80 years ago paints a much busier picture than today. Above, the scene is taken from the Church Street end with Cash's Boot and Shoe Shop on the right; they also having another branch in Alexandra Road, Six Bells. The lower photograph, was taken the same day but from the Commercial Street end.

66./67. Church Street in the 1950s and 1970s before it was semi-pedestrianised. The largest shop here was a branch of The Blaina Industrial and Provident Society (The Co-op). Virtually everything to suit the customers' needs could be purchased here, from food, electrical goods and even arrangements with the undertaker.

68. A familiar name amongst the traders of Abertillery is that of the Ash family. This picture was taken outside their original shop at No.5 Oak Street, near the old Station Hotel. The business specialised in saddlery and leather goods, catering for the needs of the main mode of transport of the period, namely the horse and cart.

69. Another well known shop was Kibby's the grocers and here are members of staff outside the premises in Somerset Street. The Kibby family were the great entrepreneurs, the business eventually developing into one of the country's leading supermarket chains. The shop is presently occupied by J & R Fashions.

70. Like most valley towns, Abertillery did not want for places of liquid refreshment, temperate or otherwise. On the right of Castle Street is The Golden Lion, to be better known these days as The Dagmar. In the background and a little further along is The Castle Inn.

71. Probably the most fashionable place in which to stay whilst visiting the town in years gone by was The Bush Hotel; in its heyday it was the flagship of the Webbs Brewery Company at nearby Aberbeeg. Now closed as licensed premises, the building is used as a rehabilitation centre for young transgressors.

72. A picture that is almost a hundred years old at the time of publication of this book. It shows The Old Bridgend at Penybont, the long-term landlord of which was Mr. Ben Fieldhouse.

73. Two business premises seen here in High Street in the 1960s have since moved on. The shop next to the bank was D. Edwards and Son, the ironmongers. Pictured shortly after opening, the ironmongers was originally yet another town hotel, The Prince Of Wales.

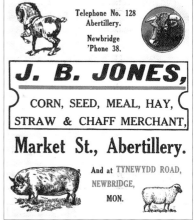

74. In Church Street during the late 1960s, are three members of the staff of Vernon's the grocers. Originally a branch of Pegler's, the premises have seen many changes of ownership since. The ladies seen here, left to right are Bonnie Lewis, Marion Lawrence and Jen Holborn.

75. This picture was taken a little further down the street from the scene in photograph number 73. It shows another disappeared retailer, Masters the clothiers who traded at the corner of The Arcade for more than seventy years; the shop is now a popular florist's.

76. Members of the local Prudential Assurance staff are pictured during an outing to London during the 1960s. There are 49 faces on the photograph in total and here are just a few to test the memory. Brian Mathias, Joyce Moore, Ray Moore, Mr. and Mrs. Gwyn Evans, Joan Harvey, Harold Vowles, Derek Hooper, Stan Bridgwater, Les Evans, Dennis Edwards, Alan Goodenough, Cherry Taylor, Mary Cox, Laura Williams and Addie Prewett.

77. On the left is Mr. George Heal, accompanied by his assistant Mike Spencer with their van parked opposite Howell's sweet shop, which was on the corner of Commerial Street. Mr. Heal at one time worked for the local lamp-oil and hardware merchant, Mr. Parsons. He would be seen delivering his wares around the town by horse and cart, long before the luxury of a van such as seen here.

78. The Arcade once housed a host of shops selling a wide variety of goods. Seen here are two ladies from Turners the shoe retailer in 1961, Miss Sweet and Miss Donaldson.

79. A scene at Church Street during the 1950s showing the shop of George Alfred Moxley, said by many to have been Abertillery's finest tailor. Moxley's and neighbouring Masters were held in high esteem particularly during the Six Bells Pit disaster. The shops, as part of their respect supplied black ties free of charge to the many mourners of those lost in the tragedy.

80. Church Street as seen from the opposite end compared with the previous photograph. The year is 1960 and here are a few shops that once served the town: Jones's Corn Shop, Tom Evans the jewellers, John Bull, Olivers for shoes, The Home and Colonial for groceries, Joseph and Faulkman and Edwards the ironmongers.

81. The County Garage, a former family-run business in Oak Street, aptly named after the nearby County School. The upper part of the garage was originally a billiard hall, with the basement being used as a stable by the Salt family, local coal-level owners. The building was acquired by Mr. Frank Adams in the early 1930s, just when motor cars were becoming a way of life, it being converted into a motor repair shop and petrol station. Petrol pumps were a novelty at this time, with motorists generally having to buy their petrol in pre-filled cans. Frank is seen in the doorway whilst a representative from one of the petrol companies demonstrates one of the latest electric fuel pumps, filling a 'Standard Ten' car. Frank Adams passed away in 1953, the business being carried on by his son Len, later to be joined by his uncle, Gwyn. The picture here was taken before major alterations, the building now housing car showrooms.

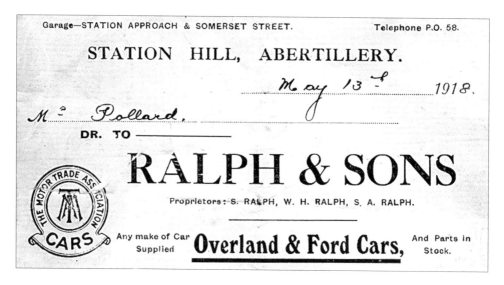

Garage—STATION APPROACH & SOMERSET STREET.   Telephone P.O. 58.

STATION HILL, ABERTILLERY.

May 13 th 1918.

Mr Pollard.

DR. TO ————

RALPH & SONS

Proprietors: S. RALPH, W. H. RALPH, S. A. RALPH.

THE MOTOR TRADE ASSOCIATION — CARS

Any make of Car Supplied   **Overland & Ford Cars,**   And Parts in Stock.

CHAPTER 4

Religious Matters

82. The Salvation Army with its adage 'Blood and Fire' was founded in the year 1865, and is now a worldwide organisation that has stood the test of time. The local movement was started in Abertillery in 1883, following the successes of the corps at nearby Blaina a year or two earlier. Captain Robinson and Lieutenant Hodges were assigned to prepare the opening work with Staff Captain Jonah Evans conducting the first meetings; the District Officer at the time being Major Coombs. As with most new religious organisations, the beginnings were humble, through lack of funds and Abertillery's first services were held in an unlikely venue, the club rooms belonging to the old Castle Hotel at the bottom of Hill Street; it is quite possible that this may have been regarded as the ideal place to start rescuing some 'lost souls'.

There was a certain amount of criticism at the time, particularly from the local Press, expressing its concern at the Army's methods of spreading the Gospel. The leaders were not deterred however and the Castle rooms were packed night after night with followers; in fact the first public tea that was arranged to help promote the cause, attracted a crowd of 700 people.

After some two years without a place of their own, the corps eventually secured a piece of land at the top of Hill Street and so a permanent hall was built; General William Booth, the Army's founder, was personally invited to perform the official opening ceremony. General Booth was to visit the town again in 1907, this time drawing an audience of more than 10,000 and bringing Abertillery to a standstill.

Captains Ron and Glenna Hughes were appointed to Abertillery in 1996 and under their leadership the corps has continued to flourish; the hall having undergone major renovation and refurbishment with increased facilities, all testimonial to the good work of the Army in the town.

The photograph seen here is of Mr. and Mrs. Veal with their daughter Alberta. Mr. Veal was bandmaster for many years, the post being carried on to this day by his grandson Graham.

83. A traditional Whitsun Walk by parents and children is in progress in 1970. They are seen here walking through Church Street on their way to the Salvation Army rooms for the customary tea. The two youngsters nearest the camera are Mark Cole on the left and Gina Williams on the right. Also to be seen are Eryl Dykes, Chris Budd, Margaret Jones, Sylvia Phillips, Lyndon and Kathryn Budd and Mrs. Lizzie Evans.

84. Another Whitsun Walk is being led by the pupils of Blaenau Gwent Baptist Chapel. It was routine for the children to parade around the town in their 'Sunday Best' and congregate at the cenotaph, with the crowds from the many other churches and chapels who joined in the march. The long walk back would be rewarded with a high tea in the Sunday School. Four young ladies seen on the right are Pam Withers, Kath Smith, Suzanne Combstock and Jackie Combstock.

85. Blaenau Gwent Baptist Church with its adjacent Sunday School buildings in about 1920.

The Early Baptists of Blaenau Gwent

Baptist worship at Blaenau Gwent can be traced back almost 350 years, much of the credit being due to the founder of the movement in South Wales, John Myles; he was widely respected as 'The Apostle of the Baptists in Wales'. In 1646, one Ambrose Mostyn came to preach the word at nearby Blaina, only to be met with a most hostile reception from the established churchgoers; at one such open-air service he was pelted with some most-unusual missiles namely dead hedgehogs and forced to flee to Gelli Crug, where he was to find a much more civilised welcome. Mostyn's teachings were fervently received and followed by the local comunity, and so, nonconformity gained its first foothold in Abertillery; the Baptists establishing themselves at Blaenau Gwent and the Independents tending to congregate at Gelli Crug. There then followed a period of relative acceptance of nonconformism throughout the country until the return of Charles II in 1660. With him, came a renewed persecution of those who declined to accept the creed of The Church of England.

Some two thousand ministers of religion were evicted from their churches, buildings were destroyed and imprisonment was commonplace. Amidst all this turmoil however, Blaenau Gwent managed to survive, due probably to its relative seclusion on a Welsh mountainside. By 1689 though, all was to change yet again with the passing of The Tolerance Bill which allowed limited freedom of worship; by now however, good preachers were few and far between thanks to the previous purges. There was but one more period of concern however in 1714, when a new Bill was introduced, ultimately intent on outlawing nonconformist religion once and for all but, due to the untimely death of Queen Anne and a change of government, it never received the required Royal signature. Thus at last the liberty of worship became an established fact. Those who held on to their faith at Abertillery were to be rewarded. Under the leadership of local bridge-builder William Phillips, the first church was constructed at Blaenau Gwent in the year 1715, a building which was to stand until 1839. By now congregations had steadily increased and the rebuilding and enlargening of the chapel became necessary. Much of this increase in the number of worshippers consisted of English immigrants, who were now flocking to the valley in search of work. So, on January 1st 1882, another landmark was reached in the chapel's history; the Sunday service was delivered in the English language for the first time!

The great religious revival came in 1904, bringing with it a surge in congregation numbers. The old chapel was now declared to be far too small and the much larger premises were built, as seen on the photograph above. This building was to last for some 80 years before being replaced by the completely redesigned church that we know today.

55

86. Sunday School scholars belonging to Blaenau Gwent have just crossed Foundry Bridge and about to make their way along Church Street. The event is a Whitsun march probably held in the late 1950s or early 1960s.

87. Some members of Blaenau Gwent Church and they are, left to right Back Row: David Hutchings, Cyril Lane, Ivor Lane, Harry Williams and Alan Davies. Front: Bill Symonds, Ray Hutchings, Rev. J.O.G. Brown, Jack Williams and Miss Gillingham.

88. Ebenezer Baptist Chapel as it appeared in the year 1877.

Ebenezer Baptist Church - The First 50 Years

Ebenezer Chapel is another pillar amongst the long-surviving structures of Abertillery's faithful. The innauguration dates from the year 1876, the year in which the ecclesiastical parish was formed. Following some disagreements at King Street Baptist Chapel, some eighty members led by Reverend Llewellyn Jones of Swansea, decided it was time to leave King Street and form a separate church of their own. Having little or no resources with which to begin, they took temporary accommodation in the old Primitive Methodist Chapel in Castle Street. The essential baptisms were conducted in the open air, firstly at the old Vivian Brickyard and later, during the winter period, at Club Row Penybont; on this occasion it is recorded that the ice had to be broken to allow the ceremony to proceed!

Gradually the members established themselves as a strong body of worshippers and considered ways of constructing their own building. A site was chosen at Park Place, an area of the town yet to be developed. Much of the labouring and digging of the foundations was carried out by the members themselves, with financial support coming from a number of private sources. One such benefactor was Mr. Moses Thomas who mortgaged his property to help fund the project. The vestry was completed in 1877 and the chapel itself was opened in April 1878. There then followed years of steady progress although not entirely without the odd financial worry, which nevertheless always found a solution. In 1904, a piece of land adjacent to the main building was purchased to erect a new lecture hall. Officially opened on August 20th 1905, the hall housed 22 classrooms and could accommodate 1000 scholars, to be taught by 34 teachers; the staggering cost, for the era, was more than £1900. This period was the zenith of religious instruction for the young, never to be repeated. The Great Welsh Revival, which had been launched in the Swansea area in November 1904 soon swept the principality and so, to the chapels they flocked. Ebenezer benefited greatly from these boosted congregations and their financial contributions, enabling the clearing of all the church debts and also the purchase of a house for the pastor.

The Great War came in August 1914 and a cloud of doom shrouded the whole of Abertillery for four long years. Ebenezer was instrumental in sending parcels of food and clothing to the troops and sailors on active service. In 1922 a War Memorial Organ and a tablet were installed in the church to honour those lost. The 1920s heralded another period of economic uncertainty for the church and the whole of Abertillery. Post-war depression hit the valley, accompanied by The General Strike of 1926 and men left in their hundreds in search of a better way of life. To end the first fifty years at Ebenezer, a small extract from some recorded minutes of a meeting held on Sunday September 20th 1925 makes poignant reading - *"It was resolved that we grant the application of the Free Church Council for the use of our Church all day on 30th September (Wednesday) for the purpose of holding a united prayer meeting for the purpose of petitioning God that the industrial cloud which hangs so heavily upon our town may be lifted".*

89. Whitsun 1963 and the ladies of Ebenezer are making the traditional walk or 'turnout' as it was often referred to.

EBENEZER
Baptist Church, Abertillery.

𝔅roadcast
𝔖ervice.

Sunday, April 22nd, 1934,
at 8 p.m.

Preacher :

REV. E. T. SAMUEL
Pastor.

Choirmaster   -   Mr. Edward Morgan.
Organist   -   Miss May Morgan.

90. From about 1982 and pictured outside Ebenezer Chapel, Rev. Paul Davies is surrounded by a young flock. Amongst the flock are Michael Jarrett, Tanya Francis, Lisa Williams, Alison Parsons, Emma Williams, Samantha ?, Sharon Davies, Lisa Randall, Nicola Pike, Angela Jarrett, Cheryl Price, Dawn Price, Richard Lloyd, Paul Randall, Kathryn Dykes, Julie Upcott, Rebecca Hunt, Nicola Randall, Kirsty Pike and Matt Williams.

91. An opportunity to view the interior of St. Michael's Parish Church some eighty years ago when Reverend Hiram Rees was vicar. The original church was constructed in the year 1854, then completely re-built of stone, in the early English style in 1898. Congregations continued to expand and by 1906 the church was further extended to accommodate 850 sittings.

92. St. Paul's Anglican Church which was built as a chapel of ease to Abertillery between 1888 and 1890, on land donated by The South Wales Colliery Company; the official opening taking place in January 1891. With sittings for 305 worshippers, it is of early Gothic design and constructed of red sandstone, which was extracted from the former quarries at Gilwern with stone tracery from the Forest of Dean.

93. Here are some members of the Red Brick Chapel's Sunday School at the top of Winifred Terrace Cwmtillery, in about 1937. To test the memory, a few names have been recalled as follows - Bert, Cynthia and Gwen Stapleton, Tony Davies, Geoffrey Davies, Val Perkins, Olive Hale, Jean and Mrs. Meredith, Maureen James, Marilyn Holmes, Vera Bateman, Jim Tippins, Doreen Williamson and Edith Davies.

94. Somerset Street Methodist Chapel which had stood for a hundred years.

Born out of 18th Century Wesleyanism, the Primitive Methodists established themselves in about 1812, the movement finding support in Abertillery between 1841 and 1844. During these early years, local services were pioneered by a William Fairclough who would travel from Nelson to preach the word. Recently having taken residence at Brynmawr from Herefordshire, was one Thomas Preece and soon he was seen as a leader who could further the cause in the Abertillery area. Despite a certain resistance to this latest model of English nonconformism, Preece took up the challenge and moved to Abertillery. He resided at Old Court Farm, Cwmnant-y-groes which soon became home for the Methodists. As the numbers grew, two other old farms, Pant-y-Pwdyn and Pant-y-Arael were utilised as houses of prayer. The next important landmark was January 1849, with the opening of the first Methodist Chapel in Castle Street. The population of Abertillery at this time was just 1200 but now on the verge of enormous expansion. Immigrants from adjoining counties and across the border came to participate in the new industrial developments, bringing too, social and moral standards of a very low order in the opinions of local religious leaders. The time was ripe for reform and renewed rigorous evangelical efforts. Amidst all this, the Methodists saw fit to erect a new chapel in the town, the site chosen being Somerset Street. This church was opened in 1876 at a cost of £1550 and heralded more than a century of service. The 'Cause' was now well and truly established yet despite later extensions, this chapel still failed to cope with demand; consequently it was decided to build a sister church in Newall Street, this opening in 1906.

By 1914 the Somerset Street building had received further improvements with the addition of a lecture hall and vestries making it one of the most commodious chapels in the town. The 1930s, a well-documented period, ushered in some familiar events, 1934 seeing the closure of Newall Street. Somerset Street however continued exceptionally well, successfully managing all its finances and congregations through the depression and war years. Unfortunately the 1970s changed all that and the church succumbed to the modern age, finally closing in 1978 and since demolished.

There is however one major remnant of this one-time Methodist Chapel still surviving, the all-important pipe organ. This ancient instrument has found its way to a church in the State of Texas, USA and that bit of history will be recorded in Volume Two of this Abertillery book.

95. The Primitive Methodist Chapel which once stood on West Bank Cwmtillery, this particular photograph dating from the year 1912. Primitive Methodism in the Abertillery district began life in the early 1840s. Following highly successful indoctrinations in the nearby Eastern Valley town of Blaenavon, the leaders cast their eyes over the hills into the Western parts of Monmouthshire; the first Methodist Chapel in Abertillery opening in Castle Street in 1849.

Cwmtillery was sparsely populated at this time and enthusiasm for yet another nonconformist doctrine was moderate. Following years of 'cottage worship', the Primitive Methodists built their first chapel at West Side in 1872, on land as yet unspoiled by the wastes of coal mining. Accommodating some 120 followers, the building was, as to be expected, soon to become inadequate and by 1887 the chapel was enlarged and an adjoining schoolroom added as seen in this photograph. By 1905 however, it was noticed that the two buildings were breaking away from each other, undoubtedly caused by the underground workings now taking place. In 1910 the chapel was finally abandoned and the devotees were obliged to make use of a local school for almost three years.

The financial position of the Methodists was not favourable and during this three-year period, campaigning was relentless to secure sufficient funds to build a new place of worship. Members themselves laboured in dismantling the old chapel, selling the unwanted timber but re-dressing the stone for use in the new. All the hard work finally came to fruition in the Spring of 1913 with the laying of the foundation stone. Progress was swift thereafter, with monies accumulating from a variety of sources, including support from local colliery operators The Lancaster Steam Coal Co. The completed chapel officially opened its doors on October 29th 1913 and enjoyed many years of success until the 1960s. The ever so repeated pattern of decline began and Cwmtillery Primitive Methodist Chapel finally closed its doors in July 1971. The site of this old chapel is now occupied by a number of bungalows for the elderly.

CHAPTER 5

People and Special Events

96. The gentleman seen here is pictured amidst the great landslip at Cwmtillery which took place in February 1913. Following torrential winter rains, the mountainside just above the colliery gave way and thousands of tons of earth and rock descended. Fortunately, the slip was gradual and local residents were able to evacuate their homes in time. Whilst there was no loss of life, a number of ancient buildings were destroyed. Ty Doctor Farm, White House (the historic meeting place of early nonconformists) and part of Top Row were victims. The whole scene attracted thousands of visitors to the area, it being anticipated that Cwmtillery's colliery was also to be consumed; subsequently the avalanche came to a quiet end as Spring arrived.

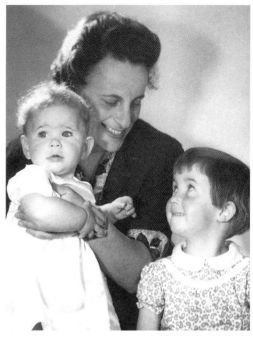

97./98. Familiar to many former patients will be the faces of Doctors Donald and Maria MaClean, seen here with children Jeannie and Ruth. Donald MaClean, a Scotsman came to Abertillery after serving with the Palestine Police and practiced in the town from 1950 until 1974. His wife Maria also practiced in Abertillery and Blaina and served as anaesthetist in several hospitals. Dr. Maria died in 1965 and Dr. Donald in 1974.

99. The year is thought to be 1958 and the scene is set outside the Houses of Parliament. The crowd here are residents of Gelli Crug, who travelled to London for the day by train from Abertillery. They were met at Westminster by their Member of Parliament at the time, Mr. Llewellyn Williams who served the Abertillery constituency from 1950 until 1965.

100. Abertillery's War Memorial was unveiled by Field Marshall, The Viscount Allenby on December 1st 1926. Allenby was an outstanding commander of British Forces in Flanders and Palestine and it was considered a great honour to receive such a distinguished soldier to perform the ceremony; he is seen here, leaving The Bush Hotel following a civic luncheon to mark the occasion. The gentleman wearing the top hat is Mr. William Brace, the former Abertillery M.P. and President of the South Wales Miners' Federation. The First World War came to an end in 1918 but, such was the economic plight of the citizens of Abertillery at the time, it was some eight years before sufficient funds could be raised to build the cenotaph.

101. The unveiling service was conducted by Rev. W.L. Harris, vicar of Abertillery, and a special film of the event was launched at The Metropole Cinema in Market Street. Intended as a memorial to those lost in World War One, 443 names were inscribed on the plaques. Unfortunately however, the names of a further nine were later discovered but omitted from the tablets. New plaques, naming 158 victims of World War Two were unveiled by the Lord Lieutenant of Monmouthshire, Lord Raglan on Sunday November 7th 1954.

Roll of Honour Abertillery & District
World War Two 1939-1945

R.G. Alexander	F.A. Hughes	C.B. Price
W. Andrews	W.J.E. Hughes	P.A. Price
W.H. Ball	W.T. Hurl	D.J. Pritchard
V. Banks	R. Hurley	N.G. Prosser
J.S. Bateman	J. Hutton	K.G. Rathbone
G. Bert	A.F. James	R. Richards
S. Blanchard	R. James	L.G. Roberts
U. Boleslaw	R.D. Jarrett	A.I. Sargeant
B. Bourne	R.O. Jasper	E. Sheppard
G.H. Brookes	B. Jenkins	J. Short
I.H. Bullett	C. John	J. Simmonds
A.E.S. Burgham	D. Jones	E. Smith
T.J. Burgham	J.C. Jones	H. Smith
R.R. Byard	J.D. Jones	W.R.L. Smith
F. Cairns	R. Jones	V.G. Talbot
A. Carter	R.J. Jones MM	R. Tarrant
R.C. Carter	R.J. Jones (Derby Rgt)	B.B. Taylor
B. Christian	T.J. Jones (RAF)	G.L. Thomas
E. Compton	T.J. Jones (RAOC)	R. Thomas
W. Cox	W.G. Jones	A.H. Tidey
N.R.J. Davey	W.J. Jones	F. Toghill (RA)
F. Davies	W.L. Jones	F. Toghill (RAF)
N.A. Davies	M.C. Kinnersley	J. Tucker
T.J. Davies	I. Lane	C. Vaughan
W.J. Davies	S. Lane	N.S. Vaughan
W.R. Deacon	E.J. Leigh	C.D.R. Verrier
H.J. Donald	A.J. Lewis	W. Verrier
E.T. Eady	J.L. Lewis	K. Viscount
G. Easley	W.J. Lewis	W. Viscount
D.J. Edmonds	W.H. Lloyd	W. Ware
G. Edmunds	J. Lowry	W.G. Ware
R.J. Edwards	E.T. Mann	P. Walbyoff
R.G. Elkins	A.G. Mason	J.P. Waters
L. Evans	C. Meredith	J.C. Webster
C.P. Frowen	J.H. Meredith	L. Weston
W.H. Gaudern	W.F. Moon	W. Whelton
H.J. Giblett	H.J. Morgan	A. White
E. Gill	T. Morgan	J.S. Whitehead
F.R. Gilson	G. Morley	E.G. William
R. Gould	L.E. Morris	A. Williams
K.G. Gwilliam	B. Nash	D.R. Williams
W.H.J. Gwilliam	E. Nash	E.A. Williams
R. Hall	L. Nash	G.A. Williams
A. Hancock	D. Nunnerley	G. Williams
R.P. Harris	G.C. Owen	H.G. Williams
W.H. Harris	H. Owen	I. Williams
R.J. Hart	F.A. Padmore	R. Williams
G.M. Higgins	C.F. Painter	F.J. Willimot
A.J. Hodder	W.G. Palmer	M.W. Wood
T.E. Hookings	T.B. Parr	A.C. Wright
S.D. Hopkin	E. Pocock	L. York
A. Howells	R. Powell	A.I .Young
E. Howells	W.A. Powell MM	

The fallen of World War Two who are listed above, served their country on land, sea and air. Lack of space unfortunately has prevented the detailing of their rank and division of the services and consequently their names are listed in pure alphabetical order.

102. The Drill Hall which was opened in about 1906, during a period of relative peace for the nation, following the end of The Boer War in South Africa in March 1902. By 1908 it was decided to consolidate the many Militia units around the country and so the familiar Territorial Army was formed. Abertillery's Drill Hall became home to a Company of The 3rd Battalion, The Monmouthshire Regiment; this inscription can be seen over the main doorway. During the 1939-45 War, the building was used by another well known band of soldiers, The Home Guard. The hall has been occupied by a number of units over the years and despite continual reorganisation and uncertainties within the T.A., it received a complete re-fit in 1987 with the exception of the main front wall. This was considered to be of important historical value for high up, can still be seen a Regimental Badge with Battle Honour 'South Africa 1901'. Today's military occupants are a Troop of 104 AD Regiment, Royal Artillery.

103. In about 1960, the lads and mascot are pictured in what was then 'P' Battery Office at the Drill Hall and they include - Front: Reg Davenport, Dick Williams, Len Adams, Fred Mannister (Regular Sgt. Major), Bill Jenkins and Tom Tyler. Back: Bob Nash, unknown, Ron Hathaway, Len Williams, Roger Hamond, unknown, George Cole, Phil McDonough and Mel Penny.

104. On the left is just one of the town's many war heroes, 2nd Lt. Cyril Salt, only son of Mr. and Mrs. Thomas Salt of Gwentland House, Oak Street, former owners of some local coal drifts. Cyril Salt together with a few of his colleagues volunteered for overseas service in September 1914, shortly after the outbreak of war. He joined the 3rd Monmouthshire Regiment and after initial training was posted to France in January 1915. Sadly during the major battle of Neuve Chapelle on March 15th, whilst only 20 yards from the safety of his trench, he received a bullet wound to the head and died in a casualty clearing station on April 3rd. Abertillery was saddened at the news of one of its first casualties, which was reported in The Times newspaper a week later; the family were devastated at losing an only son aged just 21. As in the rules of conflict, his body was not brought home and lies buried in Bailleul Cemetery, northern France.

'When sorrows come they come not single spies but in battalions' (Hamlet)

105. In 1936 the country was ruled by three different monarchs, the most contoversial probably being King Edward VIII. Wearing a bowler hat, he is seen here at the park on 19th November 1936 being introduced to a selected band of Abertillery colliery workers. The visit to the town was included as part of his tour of the depressed areas of South Wales and those memorable words, 'something must be done' were uttered. A month later he was succeeded as sovereign by his brother King George VI.

106. Anyone who might have worked for, or travelled on Ralph's Buses the former Abertillery company, will remember a few faces here. The occasion is an Annual Staff Dance held at the Drill Hall and amongst those present are - Ivor Evans, Mr. and Mrs. Jack Eason, Mr. and Mrs. Ron Screen, Charlie Smith, Eddie Harvey, Mr. and Mrs. Idris Adams, Mr. and Mrs. Windsor Caswell, Mrs.Vi White, Mr. Matthews, Mrs. Pritchard and George Michael.

107. The children seen in this Nativity Play will now be in their 'forties' and pleased to remember times at Blaentillery Infants' School in 1962. The players include, Back: Judith Blake, Jeffrey ?, Johnny Coles, Amanda Lewis, Audrey Winnett, Kim Blanchard, David Scott and Kay Marshman. Front: David Bowd, Alan Wedge, Paul Winston, Lesley Prior, Linda Owen, Alan Owen, Martin McBurnie and Clive Edgell.

108. Unfortunately space does not permit the listing of the ladies' names on this occasion but, they are members of Ebenezer's Sisterhood who are on a day's outing in 1954.

109. The customary Sunday School trip to Barry Island is recorded here in August 1966. Amongst the group from Brynteg Chapel are Philip Webber, Mike Lewis, Mark Merchant, Lorraine Morris, Pamela Tippins, Jackie Lewis, Gaynor Stingemore, Jane Price, Ann Lawrence, Kevin Webber and Julie Jones.

110. The 53-strong Male Voice Choir during their participation in the annual and ancient Marymass Festival at Irvine Scotland in 1992, the Festival itself having been celebrated for a thousand years. With the choir are Martin Budd - Musical Director; Joy King - Accompanist and Ron Protheroe - Chairman. To ensure a true Welsh flavour, in attendance are some well-attired ladies and on the left are Ann Mason and Chrissie Budd with Jean Hunt on the far right.

111. A parade through Somerset Street is in progress with a troop of scouts and their leaders. On the far right are Dorothy and Ted Meredith who have been lifelong supporters of the local Scout Movement. In the background can be seen the former Methodist Chapel.

112. A photograph which was taken during an ever popular carnival event around the town. Maybe some readers will be able to identify some of the participants or onlookers seen here?

113. The acclaimed musical director of Abertillery, Maurice David with accompanist Jean Davies in 1971. Maurice died in November 1981 and his passing was marked by a memorial service in St. Michael's Church. In remembrance of his services to the local musical fraternity, a Bishop's carved oak chair was presented to St. Michael's.

Abertillery Amateur Dramatic Society

The Abertillery Amateur Dramatic Society was created at a meeting held in The Snowdon Temperance Hotel and Cafe in Carmel Street (The Sports Club nowadays) in the year 1916. These were days when entertainment was confined to silent films in the odd cinema around the country, and perhaps the luxury of a wind-up gramophone or piano in the home; the Music Halls were in their prime. Abertillery Society's first performance was given to a rapturous audience at The Metropole Theatre in October 1916, the chosen production being Gilbert and Sullivan's ever-popular Mikado with Mr. M.E. Thomas as musical conductor. That performance marked the beginning of a long and successful history of the Society, with the month of October eagerly awaited as an annual performance was launched at The Metropole. Plays were also a popular feature in earlier years before musicals became the vogue.

Shows continued with full gusto under the leaderships of Luther Evans and Albert Price until the outbreak of war in 1939. Unfortunately 'the show did not go on' and the Society was forced to hibernate for nearly twelve years; the last presentation being a patriotic performance of Merrie England. The pre-war years saw economic depression fall particularly hard on the Abertillery district, and The Dramatic Society was to come to the aid of many in need through their voluntary concerts. Such charitable causes as The Abertillery Distress Fund, The Children's Boot Fund and The District Hospital were all grateful recipients.

It was 1951 before the Society was re-formed and their first production was The Pirates Of Penzance at The Workmen's Hall Llanhilleth. For some years thereafter, the Society performed at The Pavilion Abertillery until the grand re-opening of The Metropole in March 1962, which is where they are to this day. It was during this period that the much-talented Maurice David became musical director, serving for some 24 years. His career began at a very early age by becoming the accompanist to a local male voice choir at just fourteen. Whilst overseas during the war, he was to rub shoulders with a number of show-biz personalities and became director of a renowned Concert Party formed by Jack Hawkins, the great 1950s film star.

There are many names to mention of those who have served and supported the Society so well, for so long; enough to complete a book of its own. For instance there is Jack Wells and his wife Melba, each having served for more than forty years and Shirley Winmill, whose involvement is comprehensive. Should there be a second volume of this Abertillery book then the story will be continued.

114. The year is 1961 and seen above are the performers of The Dramatic Society in their costumes for the production of The Student Prince. The stars are - Back Row: Ann Ridout, Shirley Winmill, Sheila Morris, Gwyn Morris, Ann Morris, unknown, Sheila Abraham, Ms. Vaughan and Pam Cordy. Front: Betty Warrender, Jeanette Langley, Elaine Humphries and Susan Lawrence.

115. Another photograph from the 1960s and on this occasion the tartan dress indicates the performance to be Brigadoon. Pictured left to right are - Back: Alan Thomas (Chiefy), Jack Brickell, John Gifford, Harry Smith and Cyril Howarth. Front: Royston Sterry, Martin Cook, Philip Davies and Bill Grindle.

116. The cast of The Music Man, and here is the list of artistes to spot in this scene. Back Row: Sheila Gallier, Sheila Abraham, Alison Davies, Cynthia Vaughan, Linda Haycock, Val Rosser, Diane Jones, Lesley Bradley, Marlene Waters, Helen Pettet, Jackie Smith, Dawn Protheroe, Pat Jones, Iris Hinds and Carol Edwards. Front: Bill Hinds, Mervyn Evans, Susan Williams, Harry Jones and Cyril Howarth.

117. This time it's the turn of the 'Back Room Boys and Girls' to be acknowledged at The Metropole and they include - Trevor Winmill, Ken Winmill, Peter Rosser, Alan Smith, Joe Meadows, Ken Gilbert, Ivor White, Edgar Davies, Robert Griffiths, Susan Hewitt, Dave Howells, Harry Burrows, Graham White and Martin Henley.

118. Members of Abertillery Orpheus with some familiar faces to see as follows. Back Row: D. Emanuel, G. Baker, B. Jones, K. Crook,G. Matthews, C. Samuels, K. Rodman, T. Berrows, W. Morris, R. Protheroe and W. Ford. Third Row: H.Williams, P. Jones, D. Thomas, V. Thomas and I. Evans. Second Row: T. Wilde, W.R. James, H. Jones, J. Taylor, W. Gatehouse, H. Mathias, A. Davies, A. Sweet, A.Westcote, W. Newbold and R King. Front: C. Wright, J. Chapel, B.R. Walters, C. Young, E. James (Secretary), Mrs. L.E. James (Conductor), W.P.L. Jones (President), Mrs. Collier Watkins (Asst. Accompanist), F. Evans (Accompanist), F. Norris and C. Williams.

119. The ladies of the Bryn Gwyn Girls' Choir are re-united and conducted by Margaret Davies during a rehearsal for a memorial concert for their founder, Mr. Cyril Blake. Cyril Blake was the highly talented and respected musician of Abertillery who formed the choir whilst a teacher at Bryn Gwyn School during the 1940s. It was to become one of Wales' leading school choirs, attracting the visits of such prominent artistes as Joan Hamond and Julie Andrews to the town. Cyril and his wife eventually settled in the U.S.A., quickly establishing a highly regarded school of music in the State of New Jersey.

120. An old familiar scene in Church Street was a Ralph's bus stood at the bus stop. The crew here are driver Bill Smith and his conductor Billy Parfitt.

121. This is a group of Abertillery musicians calling themselves Sergeant's Band, the picture dating from about 1935. The band of banjo and mandolin players was formed by Fred Sergeant, who was a winder at Cwmtillery Colliery and also a popular music teacher. He is sat in the front row and to his left are Katy Ann Sergeant (daughter), Billy Owen and Len Sergeant (son). Unfortunately only one name can be remembered at the back, that of Fred Micheli who is third from the left.

122. Abertillery Orpheus Choir. With the guest artistes in the front are - Frank Evans, Mrs. L. Edmonds James, Mr. E. James, Mr. Blakemore, Mr. W.P.L. Jones and Trevor Wilde. The choristers include - C. Young, G. Lewis, Dave Emanuel, Des Emanuel, G. Newbold, D. Lewis, K. Crook, R. King, J. Taylor, W.R. James, K. Rodman, T. Berrows, W. Morris, W. Ford, J. Chapple, C. Wright, J. Williams, B.R. Walters, C. Samuels, P. Jones, G. Matthews, D. Cheedy, W. Gatehouse, G. Baker, W. Jones, C. Rees, H. Evans, A. Davies, A. Sweet, D. Thomas, B. Lewis, H. Jones, F. Norris, A. Westcote, R.L. Protheroe and I. Evans.

123. A collection of talented songstresses as members of the Ladies Orpheus Choir pose for a photographer.

124. Those were the days, when the butcher's boy delivered your meat order on his bike. The lad here is Bill Smith who worked for Mr. Rees the butcher, formerly of Church Street. This photograph was taken in Carlyle Street.

125. A pretty scene taken at Cwmtillery in the summer of 1962. With an abundance of attractive ladies, the village was quite capable of providing its own Carnival Queen in competition with Abertillery. Virginia Smith, the Queen of '62 is seen here with her court. From the back, left to right are - Christine Wallace, Janice Winney, Sian Llewellyn, Sonia Chandler, Alan Wedge, Linda Winnett, Judith Hart and Mervyn Stapleton.

126. Celebrations are in hand at Brynmorgan Terrace in August 1945 to mark VJ Day and long awaited peace after six years of war. Although food was still heavily rationed, the residents have managed to provide for the day. Amongst those to be seen are Bill Nash, Dorothy Jones, Mrs. Gardner, Mrs. Welsh, Ken Harding, Mrs. Atwell, Gary Adams, the Gilson twins, Mrs. Silk, Mrs. Jones, Harold Meek and John Price.

127. The Cwmtillery Carnival Queen of 1964 surrounded by her entourage. The smiling faces include - Back: Christine Wallace, Mary Clothier, Christine Woodward, Irene Clark, unknown. Front - Unknown, Sandra Stapleton, Yvonne Greenough and Andrew Downey.

128. This is the earliest known photograph of The Pavilion Theatre, the picture dating from 1907. In the background can be seen the chimney stacks belonging to the old tin works, now the site of a new supermarket.

129. A parade by the scouts down Commercial Street also provides an opportunity to see yet another building which has since disappeared from the town; it is the former Globe Inn seen here on the left.

130. From about 1955 comes this picture of a few local troops at Bude Training Range and amongst the group are C. Harvey, L. Adams, D. Sweet, R. Howells, F. Brimble and K. Bevan.

131. The traditional Nativity Play is performed at Gelli Crug School in 1963 and most of the artistes can be named - Back Row: Jane Robbins, Sharon James, Stephanie Waugh, Carol Hart, Keri Hillier and Keri Price. Middle Row: ?, Steven Simmonds, ?, ?, ?, Vivienne Coles, Neil Fowler, Alan Smart, Tony Collier, Hugh Fairclough, Michael Pagett, Clive Ellis and Janet Thay. Front: Cherie Fox, Christine Williams, Andrew Price, ?, Stephen Waugh, Andrea Edwards, Sheila Baker, Eileen Alford, Philip Hathaway, Philip Wallace and Elaine Lewis.

132. A further selection of 'would be stars' from Gelli Crug, most of whom can be named - Back: John Amphlett, Nicholas Simmonds, Andrew Churchward, Christine Williams and Julie White. Middle: ?, Carol Hart, Jane Robbins, Cherie Fox, Helen Smith, Yvonne Phelps, Brian Pitt and Andrew Collier. Front: Kevin Simmonds, Neil Fowler, ?, ?.

133. Some regulars and a particularly well-known celebrity are seen during an evening at Blaentillery Workmen's Club in 1965. The gentleman centre front is none other than film star Oliver Reed with Rose Combstock and Phoebe Thomas at his side. Sat behind are - Martha Nash, Margaret Davies, Robert Davies, Jack Wilkes, Fred Thomas, Roland Wilkes and Grace Wilkes. Blaentillery Club is a long-standing institution and celebrated its 75th Anniversary in 1997.

134. The Cwmtillery Excelsiors AFC have much to celebrate at The Top Hat Club following a highly successful season 1979/80 by the Saturday and Sunday sides. The gentlemen include - Standing: Len Greenough, David Padfield, Mark Price, Philip Roan, Steve Vranch, John Preece, Tom Summers, Chris Townsend, Dennis Flay (Capt. Saturday side), Ian Horner, David Farr, Steven Gough, Harry Thomas (First Aid), Malcolm Higgins, Jim Thomas, Mark Newman and Keith Williams. Seated: Philip Veale, Paul Preece, Paul Davies, Chris Arnold (Capt. Sunday side), Gerald Higgins, Martin McDonald, Robert Hart and Paul Richards. The mascot is Leigh Preece.

135./136. Each and everyone is entitled to a long and happy retirement and there are a number of organisations in Abertillery catering for such needs. These two photographs are of groups of Cwmtillery pensioners enjoying themselves whilst on holiday a few years ago. Notice in the upper photograph that Johnny Hicks is in the centre with his trophy, having won a talent competition with a rendering of 'Danny Boy'.

137. Amidst all the substantial industrial environment that graced the town in the nineteenth century, a magnificent twenty acre park was provided for the public. This tranquil scene which shows some ladies with fashionable headwear dates from 1905.

138. The entrance to the park as it looked during the 1920s. Over the years this section of flower beds fell into neglect, before being utilised by the building of the Remploy factory.

139. Another 1920s scene in the park showing the weir in the Ebbw Fach river; this spot is today crossed by a footbridge. Abertillery Park was established on ground originally known as Old Barn Field and purchased for development by the local council in the year 1898.

140. Two gentlemen stood at the park entrance in about 1904. Once one of the largest such parks in the valleys, it hosted many sporting activities; its superior rugby ground has also earned the respect of world class teams such as Australia and New Zealand who have played upon it over the years. Many may also remember another great annual event, the athletics meeting provided by The Monmouthshire Police Athletic Association.

141.   Another day out for the pensioners of Cwmtillery and among the crowd are
Mr. and Mrs. Taylor, Mrs. Phillips, Doll Holmes, Mr. and Mrs. Westacott, Mrs. Tyler,
Bill Bennett and Tom Higgins.

142.   The Amateur Dramatic and Musical Society in March 1986 with the following
stars to be seen. Back: Huw Jones, Harry Jones, Jack Wells, Peter Pratt, Alan Jones,
?. Fourth Row: Robert Ashmead, Bill Hinds, John Gifford, ?, Robert Haycock, Huw
Rosser, Alan Thomas and Cyril Jones. Third Row: Shirley Winmill, Pat Jones, Linda
Haycock, Jeanette Saunders, Susan Gifford, Diane Jones, Iris Hinds, Caroline Sartin,
Helen Pettet, Jacqueline Price and Dawn Price. Second Row: Val Rosser, Pat Pratt,
Mary Harrhy, Sharon Austin, Melba Wells, Joyce Jones, Cynthia Vaughan, Sheila
Abraham and Sheila Gallier. Front: Sarah Butcher, Gwen Rosser, Alyson Edwards,
Lesley Bradley, Louise Haycock, Jane Gifford and Allyson Cook.

CHAPTER 6

Teachers and their Pupils

143. The former British Town Schools seen here in about 1910. Originally there was just one building for the education of boys only, it being extended a number of times in later years, catering for girls and infants. The school closed in 1987 and the buildings seen here have now been demolished and replaced by a home for the elderly.

144. Class 1Y at The British School in 1971 and being photographed are - Back Row: Miss Hammond, Gavin Gough, Stephen Morgan, Paul Watkins, Andrew Watkins, Andrew Cole, Christopher Evans, Gary Taylor and David Daley. Third Row: Mark Francis, Mark Crozier, Cindy Taylor, Elaine Donovan, Helen Cardwell, Diane Coles, Jayne Wilson, Beverley Silverthorne, Donna Bridge, Stuart Bailey and Glyn ?. Second Row: Angela Baldwin, Elizabeth Weale, Jane Pugh, Sian Roberts, Karen Sutton, Julie Beasant, Alison Owen and Angela Morgan. Front: Richard Hall, Tony Chapman, Carl Langdon, Tony Finney, Andrew Merchant, Philip Young, Shaun Meredith and Simon Cole.

145. Class 4E at Gelli Crug pose for their final photograph before leaving the school for good in 1963. Mr. Arthur Hill was their teacher at the time and the pupils here are - Back: Martin Whitcombe, Susan James, Suzanne Gait, Robert Hayward, Ann Hulme, Raymond Smith, Jennifer Williams, Carol Dean, Janice Tingle, Lynette Jones, Margaret Llewellyn, Cheryl Watkins and Ann Probert. Front: Barry Turner, Margaret Sheene, Lena Assirati, Ann Pritchard, Carol Goodway, Anita Lane, Penny Sweet, Margaret Strickland, Dorothy Padfield, Hilary Briscoe and Christine Llewellyn.

146. Gelli Crug in the 1950s with some familiar names to recall. The boys include, Clifford Evans, Graham Stott, John Love, Frank Cavaciuti, Lleon West, Gary Hume, Melvyn Hughes, Peter Davies, Barry Dean and Gerald Carpenter. The girls are, Virginia Smith, Susan Finamore, Mary Page, Marlene Hinds, Pat Crowdace, Maureen Jones, Barbara Sweet, June Wallace, Phyllis Barret Christine Snell, Beryl Gaut, Sylvia Hems and Barbara Dawkins.

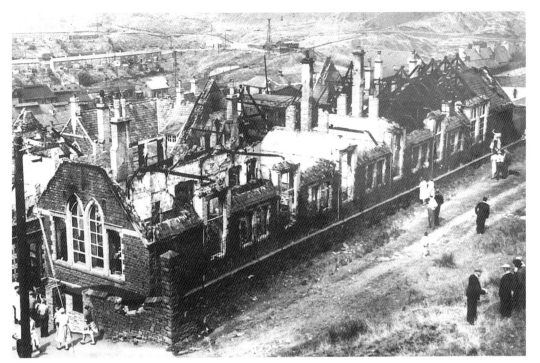

147. The onlookers are viewing the remains of the original Blaentillery School which was destroyed by fire. The site was razed to the ground and replaced by the present Infants' and Primary School.

148. A class of girls at The British School in about 1959 which includes - Back Row: Susan Whittingham, Lesley Farr, Suzanne White, Ann Butcher, Margaret Mason, Ruth MaClean, Eryl Griffiths, Stephanie Baynham, Linda Gait and Margaret Ewins. Middle: Linda Taylor, Jennifer Spencer, Carol Edwards, Sylvia Pritchard, Shirley Milkins, Carol Pritchard, unknown, Janet Alford, Linda Smith and Jane Gait. Seated: Patricia Meek, Anita ?, unknown, Gwyneth Powell, Sharon ?, Gillian Rush, Hilary Parsons, Julie Brickell, unknown and Jacqueline ?.

149. The younger members of the British School in about 1970 and to be seen are - Back: ?, Teresa Mills, ?, Sean Corrigan, Terry Mills, Michael Blanchard, Alison Waters, Lesley Biles, Ann Ford and Kay Hucker. Middle: Teresa Nicholls, Steven Duggan, Jacqueline Lewis, Mark Thorne, Carl Nicholls, ?, Dean Carpenter, Karen York and Dorothy Rogers. Front: Anthony and Andrew Rogers, Jill Brain, Debbie Richards, ?, Leslie ?, Caroline Waters, Derek Jones, Jacqueline Perrett and Jeanette Shanahan.

150. The British Juniors, Girls' School and most of the young ladies have been traced. Back: Lynne Roberts, Gillian Case, Linda Morris, ?, Christine French, Debbie Howells, Ellen Smith, ?, Lesley Ward. Second Row: ?, Helen Whittingham, Kay Rogers, Erica Edwards, Jane Aubrey, Elizabeth Gaut, Linda Hart, Karen Young, ?. Third Row: Jacqueline Brown, Julie Carter, Kathryn Huntley, Susan Wayne, Sian Edwards, Sally Wayne, Diane Morris, Lynne Francis, Dawn Morris, Keri Landers. Front: Yvonne Phelps, Gail Evans, Jane Powell, Sharon Haines, Susan Jones and Tracey Edwards.

151. Class 3A at Gelli Crug School in the late 1950s and we can see the following - Back: Christine Smith, Mary Lambert, Mary Beeze, Kay Sweet, Kay Bridge, Susan Smith, Pauline Richards, Ann Davies, Caroline Samuels, Lorraine Sweet and Pam Perrot. Third Row: Maureen Williams, Ann Mason, ?, ?, David Beddis, Brian Harvey, Edwin Morgan, Martin Meredith, ?, Gary Vaile and Eileen Griffiths. Second Row: Pat Wilcox, June Sheen, Jean Ellis, Pam Wayne, Margaret Payne, Verena Deacon, Janice Miller, Joan Pembridge, Sandra Williams and Vivienne Blake. Front: David Bird, Martin Brickell, Alan Winters, Gerald Chandler, Alan Green, David Tucker, Cyril York, ?.

152. Teachers Mr. Price and Miss Phillips with some pupils at The British School in the early 1970s. The children are - Back: Richard Hall, Michael Preece, Dawson Hulme, Andrew and Paul Watkins, Steven Fisher, Andrew Cole and Philip Young. Third Row: Simon Turner, Steven Bond, Mark Legge, Diane Coles, Carol Hughes, Debbie Hill, Donna Legge, Ian Williams, Robert Hart and Mark Blanchard. Second Row: Suzanne Blanchard, Elizabeth Butcher, Sian Roberts, Gina Williams, Kim Hollings, Keri Line, Sian Phillips and Angela Baldwin. Front: Michael Screen, Christopher Evans, Carl Langdon, Michael Prosser, David Morgan and Philip Hartwell.

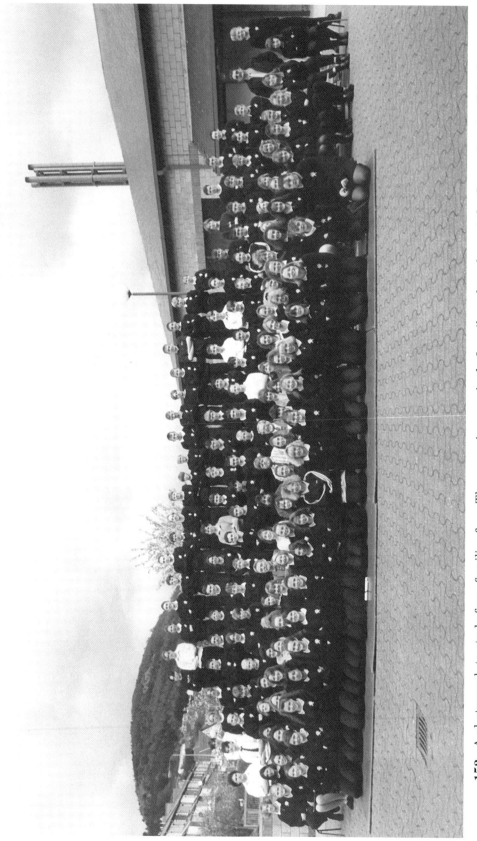

153. A photograph to study for a familiar face. The group is comprised of pupils and teachers at the Comprehensive School in 1996.

154. Queen Street Infants' School in 1960 and the pupils are accompanied by their teacher at the time, Mrs. Williams. Quite a few of the children's names have been given as follows - Back: Andrew Morris, Kevin Meredith, Chris Moss, Paul Evans, Paul Brickell and Phillip Parr. Third Row: Robert Parsons, David Collins, Barbara Green, Linda Green, Susan Willis, ?, Gary Mann, ?. Second Row: ?, Carol Edwards, Jeanette Hughes, ?, ?, ?. Front: Neil Winmill, Donald Wyatt, Ralph Morgan, ?.

155. The British Junior Girls' School, the year on this occasion is 1965 and where possible the names have been traced. Back: Belinda Stone, Linda Owen, Lynne Brooks, Julie ?, Gillian Howells, Susan Attwood, Julie Trigg, Julie Santer, Kerry Tingle, Keri Deasey and Lynne Durban. Middle: Michelle Griffiths, Coleen Cutter, Jillian Welch, Julie Mortimer, Jayne Milkins, Lynette Boulter, Julie Rickard, Fay Roberts, Beverley Mason, Anne Sellwyn, Pamela Roberts and Yvonne Ford. Front: Judith Hart, Diana Shore, Mair Lloyd, Carol Lloyd, Lynette Battle, Christine Battle, Audrey Winnett, Julie Price, Lorraine ?, Lesley Edwards, Julie Voyce and Sharon ?.

156. This time it's the boys and their teachers who are seen at The British School in 1965 and they include - Back: Mr. Bernard Cummings, Billy Price, Keith Alford, Richard Morley, John Mannell, Lyndon Edwards, Alan Owen, Nathan Davies, Philip Goulding and Mr. John Gomery. Third Row: Alan Partridge, Robert Dean, Philip York, Philip Bevan, Kelvin Stingemore, Royston Chilton, Tim Cox and Jeffrey Childs. Second Row: Leigh Jenkins, Brian Price, Tony Parfitt, Steven Vranch, Roger Gough, Jeffrey Taylor, Philip Rees and Michael Howells. Front: Des Rees, Philip Veale, Justin Edmonds, Michael Chapman, Peter Crooks, Lyn Morgan, Alan Price and Stephen Price.

157. Gelli Crug Infants dressed for the St. David's Day celebrations in 1976. Top Row: Heath Gait, Martin Phelps, Ryan Sterry, Jason Rice, Ian Lines, Paul Farr, Robert Baton, Glen Taylor, Matthew Smith, Stephen Knight, David Price and Paul Hucker. Middle Row: Sallyanne Gardiner, Clare York, Alison Parker, Roberta Jayne, Lisa Rice, Paula Holborn, Lisa Stevens, Lisa Edwards, Adrian Summers and Jonathan Tucker. Front Row: Lisa Strickland, Sharon Turner, Leighton Phillips, Simon Edmunds and Joanne Bartlett.

158. The British School in the 1970s with Miss McNeil and her pupils. Not all of the names can be traced but here are a few to look for - Back: Ann Ford, Karen York, Jacqueline Lewis and Theresa Nicholls. Middle: Dean Carpenter, Sean Corrigan, Carl Nicholls, Robert Adams, Steven Duggan and Terry Mills. Front: Jill Brain, Theresa Mills and Philip Yates.

159. Girls with their teacher at The British School and here are a few names to recall. Back: Jane Robbins, Keri Hillier, Eileen Alford, Karen Goulding, Debbie Young, Vivienne Coles, Carol Jones, Lyn Battle and Lynette Burroughs. Middle: Mair Lloyd, Sharon James, Cherie Fox, Stephanie Waugh, Andrea Edwards, Elaine Withers, Janet Thay and Keri Price. Front: Julie White, Carol Hart, Katrina Howells, Wendy Pittaway, Janet Rowles, Julia Ashman, Maxine Lloyd, ?, Suzanne Blanchard.

160./161. Both of these photographs show the former County Intermediate Grammar School, taken a few years apart. Above, the school is seen as it appeared when originally built in the year 1897. Below it is seen again, this time in 1911 when the building had been substantially extended at both ends.

162./163. The following set of six photographs were taken at the Grammar School in March 1971 and there are almost five hundred pupils and staff to be accounted for! The Headmaster at the time may be remembered as Dr. Kenneth Colombo.

164./165. The Welsh Intermediate Education Act of 1889 enabled the establishment of Abertillery's Grammar School; the original building of 1897 accommodating 70 boys and 50 girls.

166./167. The school was extended in 1911 under the headmastership of William Lewis-Evans and could now cater for a total of 260 pupils. Comprehensive education became law in the early 1980s and the title 'Grammar' was removed; closure followed and the buildings which were almost 100 years old, were finally demolished in the mid 1980s.

168. Queen Street Infants' School in 1932 and for names, this picture will test one's memory to the full. Here are some to look for - Back Row: Adolphus Hammond, Ron McCulloch, Reg Parsons, Cliff Hunt and Keith Edwards. Third Row: Royston Hocking, Fred Moyle, Alfie Turner, Barry Parr and Ivor Gifford. Second Row: Garthan James, Eileen Smith, Len Baker, Harry Banks and Don Richards. Front Row: Iris Evans, Melvyn Price, Harry Powell and Ken Peterson.

169. From the late 1950s, the girls belonging to the County School netball team are pictured in the school yard. Unfortunately on this occasion the authors have been unable to trace any of the ladies' names.

170. Rose Heyworth Comprehensive, probably during the 1970s and as not all the names have come to hand, readers on this occasion will need to test their memories. Those known include Andrew Stone, Terry Townsend, Stuart Osman, Gavin Rogers, Royston Welch, Philip Bevis, Alison Waters, Debbie Richards, Karen Richards, Ann Ford, Lyn Wilkins, Sharon Morgan, Tracy Hayman, Diane Mifflin, Caroline Walters, Caroline Turner, Ruth Crandon, Susan Simmonds, Jill Brain, Karen Thomas, Dawn Battle, Mark Thorne, Steven Duggan and Jamie McCarthy.

171. There is a certain look of innocence on this picture of a class of boys and girls at Queen Street School. It was taken in the school yard in 1958 and here are a few names to remember - Gillian Taylor, Angharrad Morgan, Gail Wookey, Marilyn Bishop, Julie Minty, Catherine Mahoney, Angela Coleman, Margaret Evans, Julie Richards, Steven Jones, Malcolm Jones, Ian and Steven Clease, Lyn Davies, Marvin Walker, Colin Poore, Kelvin Parfitt and Anthony Allen.

172. Headmistress Mrs. Pritchard and fellow teacher Miss Collett join the girls for a photograph in the yard at the British School. Not all of the girls' names can be identified but here are a few - Ann Ford, Susan Simmonds, Bev Smith, Caroline Waters, Judith Betty, Debbie Richards, Diane Mortimore, Lyn Wilkins, Tracy Edwards, Teresea Mills, Karen Lewis, Gaynor Symmonds, Keri Burgham, Jane Butcher, Linda Rees, Helen Meek, Alison Waters, Keri Finch, Sharon Davies and Sharon Morgan.

173. Gelli Crug in the 1950s and here are a few pupils' names to remember - John Sheppard, Graham Statt, Terry Williams, Alan Jones, Arthur Rowles, Julie Smith, Sandra Slaughter, Gloria Payne, June Evans, Maureen O'Keefe, Trilby Meredith, Anne Jones, Virginia Smith, Lorraine Shaw, Gloria Powell, Marjorie Bevan, Brian Taylor and Michael Jones.

CHAPTER 7

Sporting Interests

174. The ancient game of bowls is as popular with the ladies as with the gentlemen these days. Encouraged by their counterparts, The Abertillery Ladies Bowls Club was formed in 1986 with just seven members; this has now expanded some five-fold with a waiting list. The girls are seen here in 1996 with Mayor and Mayoress Ceinwen and Malcolm Dally and Dennis O'Loughglin, Director of Leisure Facilities, Blaenau Gwent.

175. Photographed on the same day in their 'Whites' are the gentlemen members of Abertillery's Club.

176. Abertillery Bowls Club was formed in the year 1911 by a group of local tradesmen, wishing to promote some relaxation on the 'green' for their fellow businessmen. Quite possibly intended for men only in those days and, of the right stature, early Club records suggest that Wednesday afternoons were a particularly popular attraction, a 'half-day' in the shopkeepers' calendar. The founders were Sidney Ash (Saddler), Jim Head (Builder), Bill Mason (Shoe Retailer) and Wattie Waters (Teacher), the latter to become a reputable International during the 1920s. The game was to gain much popularity after the end of war in 1918 and subsequently joined the Monmouthshire Bowling Association in 1924, Abertillery providing a number of Presidents over the years. Seen on this page left to right, are three Abertillery players who uniquely reached International level namely Teddy Jones, Sam Day and Cliff Hunt, all three achieving the supreme accolade of Captain of the Welsh Team.

177. These elegant-looking Abertillery bowlers are seen in 1913 having won the West Monmouth Bowling League. Reading left to right from the back they are F. Sheen, S.G. Hughes, E. Jones, S. Williams, W. Hay, J. Bailey, M. Sheen, W. Tiley, L. Blackmore, T. Beynon, W. James, G.A. Carter, W. Waters, E. Jones Williams J.P. (President), A. Simonds, R.J. Edwards, J. Wallace, E. Williams, C. Reynolds and C. Preece.

178. This is how the Bowling Green looked in the park in the 1920s and in the background, there is recreational activity of some description on the field with the old original grandstand packed to the full.

179. Long before the arrival of all-year round amenities such as Leisure Centres, outdoor swiming pools were a popular attraction in the towns, often provided by Workingmen's Funds. This is the old pool which was situated in the park, near the old Blaina Road and now long demolished.

180. Table Tennis is the game here and the players seen at Nantyglo School in about 1972 are - Back: Stephen Jenkins, Peter Hunt, Stephen Caldwell and Robert Bowen. Front: Alan Coles, Chris Hill, Mr. Jack Bland, Philip Harrhy and Andrew Jones.

181. A combined schools rugby team from the early 1930s in the capable hands of Mr. Jake Llewellyn, the boys' names unfortunately having been lost in the mists of time. Jake, now in his 'eighties' can still be seen however, walking each day from Six Bells to Abertillery doing his shopping. He is pictured here, front row, second right.

182. A young Abertillery District XV of 1952 and being some years past, it has not been possible to locate all their names. Here however are just a few for readers to recall perhaps W.H.E. Williams, John Gumbleton, Basil Mills, Roger Leyshon, Frank Jones, J. Hughes, Bob Berryman, Derek Watts, Graham Davies, D. Abraham, John Grindle, Albert Fear, Mr. Richards, Don Price and Doug Woodward. Apologies to those whose names have eluded the authors.

183. There are a few distinguished names included in this picture of the Technical School first XV taken in 1956. The line up is as follows - Back: P. Griffiths, M. Biggs, G. Jones, R. Taylor, M. Blosse, Mr. T. Powell, R. Tillings, G. Evans, J. Wilks and F. Olding. Front: G. Edwards, R. Taylor, A. Angel, Ernie Lewis (International Referee), Alan Silk (Welsh Schools Cap), Mr. J. Davies, A. Marshall, Arthur Lewis (future British Lions) and B. Collier.

184. A few years on and the boys, with a well-earned shield are pictured in the year 1963.

185. The committee members of Cwmtillery Rugby Club during the early 1960s. Some of their names can be remembered and they are - Dai Holmes, Gary Stapleton, Lloyd Owen, Denzil Davies, Graham Bartlett, Ken Hewitt, Haydn Gibson, Dolly Holmes, Sylvia Davies, Mr. Spencer, Brian Coleman, Mrs. Gibson and mascot Jeffrey Taylor.

186. The 1948-49 season photograph and some of the names have been traced as follows. Back: W.H.E. Williams, D. Kendrick, Mr. Hatton, Campbell Watts, G. Thomas and Bert Lloyd. Front: Messers Williams, Mills, Meredith, Morgan, Lamb, Idris Price, Brinley Roberts and Alan Hunt.

187. The Grammar Technical School 2nd Rugby XV during the 1970-71 Season. Back Row: John Davies, Tonto Williams, unknown, unknown, John Duggan, David Weaver and John Green. Middle Row: Robert Poole, Gareth Hopes, Wayne Chivers, John Atkins (Captain), Mr. Ernie Lewis (Teacher) and Mark Saunders. Front: Phillip Trigg, John Cook, Phillip Makemson and Neil Winmill.

188. From the year 1909 comes this photograph of the Abertillery Harriers, including four gentlemen with the Welsh Insignia who were to represent their country. The athletes' names are as follows Back Row: F. Morgan, G. Horler, J. Dix, J. Phillips, W.J. Little, A. Chaplin, G. Goode, B. Bodenham and W. Strickland. Third Row: M. Cox, T. Dukes, L. Pavey, J. Meredith, L. Evans, E.J. Thomas, J. Newton, W. Clayton, A. Williams, H. Reed and F. Tarret. Second Row: W. Pearce, W. Gulliford, D. Chiddy, W. Davies, J. Williams, G. Meredith, J. Doyle and T. Wiltshire. Front Row: W. Matthews, J. Pavey, J. Coombes, A.S. Wilson, F. Berrows, W. Clarke and A.Pope.

189. Skittles is thought to be the name of the game on this occasion, the venue being The Top Hat Club for some celebrations. The players are - Back: Charlie Thomas, Joe Stapleton, Len Perrot, Gus Kent, Edgar Warfield, Frank Screen, Bert Skeen and Ray Shepherd. Middle: H. Gibson, Fred Brimble, R. Hucker, P. Jones, Mr. and Mrs. George Jones, Bill Hughes, Bill Dixon, A. Jones and Ron Mason. Front: Jim Thomas, Des Thomas, Jack Herridge, G. Fairclough, Jim Perrot, Sam Tucker and Albert Padfield.

190. A chance to meet the Abertillery Leisure Centre Indoor Bowls Club celebrating their second consecutive victory in the Dragon League Knockout Cup in 1995. Back Row: Mel Cordy, Bryn Phillips and Sandy Morris. Seated: Monty Howells, Roy Taylor, Gary Hillier, George Crandon, Stan Thompson, Dai Lewis and Clive Daniels.

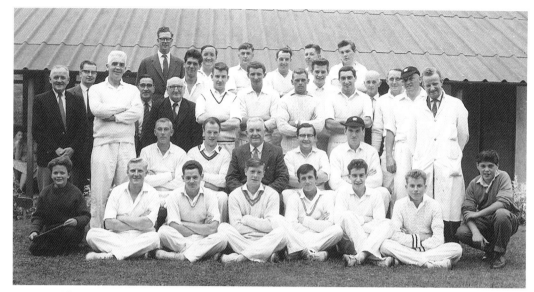

191. Abertillery Town Cricket Club is quite a mature organisation having been formed in about 1885. With a strong following, the club has developed much in recent years. The photograph above is from the 1961 season and includes the undermentioned. Back Row: H. Smith, A. Dean, R. Berryman, G. Cole, W.G.G. James and M. Williams. Second Row: R. Lee, B. Tidey, J. Mounter, F. Berryman, W. Roberts, P. Tingle, J.M. Lewis, K. Jones, K. Rossiter, R. Williams, D. Paul, D. Abraham, R. Bevan, V. Cecil and W. Kidner. Seated: A. Hayman, D. Abraham (Captain), G. Lewis (Chairman), P.T. Lewis and C. Salter. Front: D. Adams, M. Langdon, D. Brain, M. Crowley, E. Griffiths, M. Williams, M. Edwards and C. Jones.

192. The Cricket Club boasts a large collection of enthusiasts, sufficient in fact to field three League XIs on Saturdays, Sunday and Weekday XIs and also a youth section. As to be expected there are regular tours, reaching as far north as Nottingham and eastwards to London. Pictured above at a favourite venue are Back Row: C. Rogers, P. Gough, G. Edwards, C. Cooper, A. Hughes, S. Doel. Middle: C. Ellis, M. Cox, D. Clark, I. Rossiter, T. Lewis, A. Langdon, D. Abraham, G. Wilsher, G. Trapnell, S. Jones, S. Greenaway, M. Bevan, C. Jones, D. Bradley. Front: M. Shore, J. Fox (3rd XI Capt.), T. Tucker (Vice Chairman), A. Seymour (Capt.), D.G. Abraham (Treasurer), M. Probert (2nd XI Capt.), D. Morris.

CHAPTER 8

Abertillery Then and Now

The final chapter in this book is devoted to a compilation of photographs with a specific purpose in mind. That purpose is to remind those, who are old enough and can remember Abertillery 'as it used to be' and those who are not, of the startling changes that have affected the town so much as the years have passed by.

193./194. These two photographs of Foundry Bridge were taken firstly in about 1928 and then again in the Spring of 1998. The changes in scenery speak for themselves, notably the completely reconstructed bridge and the disappearance of the houses on one side of Alma Street.

195./196. A look up Alma Street in 1908 and 1998, the appearance of which is still easily recognisable, except that when the upper picture was taken, there were houses on both sides of the street. Even at the turn of the century, in most valley towns there was a certain class distinction to be noticed by the quality of abode available; quite cynically, Alma Street was to earn itself the nickname of 'Posh Street'!

197./198. The development of the town continues as to be seen here. The main building in view was The Station Hotel and since converted into Abertillery's Rugby Club. This area changed completely after the closure of the railway station which is just visible on the left of the upper photograph.

199./200. Probably the busiest street in the town, High Street as seen some eighty years apart. Although the prominent buildings would have changed hands many times over the years, they are still recognisable in the year 1998.

201./202. Church Street and once upon a time Number 18 belonged to the chain of valley grocers Peglers, with quite a large number of staff as seen above. When the lower photograph was taken in 1998 the premises and staff had taken on a completely new look, that of a popular hairdressing salon.

203./204. Once the main Post Office in the town this building has seen a number of uses including that of a popular cafe. The main structure on the corner of High Street is much the same today although some new buildings have been added alongside.

205./206. Two views looking up Commercial Street, the periods being almost a century apart. The Midland Bank was once Edwin Price's chemist shop and from the photograph above it appears that the Arcade has yet to be opened.

207./208. Above is seen the industrial heart of the town as it looked during the early 1920s. From the same spot today all has gone, the tin works closing its doors in October 1957 and the very latest addition to be built here is a new supermarket.

209./210. The bottom end of Oak Street was once the site of the busy railway station. Without the help of the lower photograph, it would be most difficult for the younger generation to picture where the valley train service used to operate.

211./212. Two of the one-time largest shops in the town, The Bon Marché and Pontlottyn Stores are featured here on the left of Somerset Street. Still recognisable many years on, they have both now been converted into supermarkets.

213./214. A look at Somerset Street facing south in the 1920s and 1998. The large shop on the left (now a branch of Fads) was once the town's Woolworth Store before moving to its present site in High Street in 1964. In the upper picture and on the opposite side of the street was The Dorothy Cafe. It was in the upstairs room of this cafe that boistrous singing could be heard, as members of 'The Dorothy Choir' practised their musical talents. This was another of Abertillery's respected choirs whose conductor may be remembered as Jessie Hinds.

215./216. Time has lapsed more than forty years between these two views from the same spot in Oak Street. The right-hand side of the street has not changed a great deal with the exception of the gas street lamp. On the left is the shop once owned by Queenie Bradbury and next door, is the old County Garage which is now the site of the car showroom of Mr. Danny Bishop.

217./218. The final pair of photographs in this book well illustrate just what can be done in recovering former industrial wasteland. The scenes are from the west side looking towards Cwmtillery.

Acknowledgements

The authors are most grateful to the undermentioned who kindly loaned some of their original material and valuable time for the production of this book. Sincere apologies are extended to anyone who may have been inadvertently omitted due to an unintended oversight.

Mr. J. Adams, Mr. L. Adams, Mr. L. Bannon, Mr. A. Bowd, Mrs. C. Brooks, Mr. J. Coombes, Mr. C. Daniels, Mr. P. Davies, Mrs. G. Deveraux, Mrs. V. Dukes, Mr. and Mrs. K. Dykes, Mr. D. Edwards, Mr. M. Edwards, Mr. J. Fox, Mrs. J. Frampton, Mrs. J. Gait, Miss Gillingham, Mr. and Mrs. W. Griffin, Mr. C. Hill, Mrs. J. Holborn, Mr. M. Howells, Mr. A. Hucker, Mr. C. Hunt, Mrs. S. Jones, Mr. M. Lewis, Mr. J. Llewellyn, Mrs. M. Lowman, Mrs. J. MaCallum, Mr. E. Meredith, Mrs. M.E. Oakley, Mrs. L. Olding, Miss A. Owen, Mrs. R. Paul, Mrs. K. Price, Mr. R. Protheroe, Mr. G. Pullinge, Mr. D. Robins, Mrs. J. Rogers, Mr. T. Russell, Mr. B. Smith, Mr. W. Symonds, Mr. C. Taylor, Mr. E. Thomas, Mr. and Mrs. M. Thomas, Mrs. Thompson, Mr. W.H.E. Williams and Mrs. S. Winmill.